MW00629024

MOUNTAIN OF FIRE AND MIRACLES MINISTRIES

13 Olasimbo Street, off Olumo Road,
Onike P. O. Box 2990, Sabo,
Yaba, Lagos.

PRAY YOUR WAY

into

2022

**PLEASE, COME TO THE CROSS-OVER NIGHT
PRAYER MEETING WITH THIS PAMPHLET**

The Mountain of Fire and Miracles Ministries is devoted to the revival of apostolic signs, Holy Ghost fireworks and the unlimited demonstration of the power of God, to deliver to the uttermost.

At MFM churches all over the world, holiness within and without, as the greatest spiritual insecticide and a condition for heaven, is being taught openly.

MFM is a do-it-yourself gospel ministry. There, your hands are trained to war and your fingers to fight.

If you are in Lagos, join us to worship at the International Headquarters, 13 Olasimbo Street, off Olumo Road, Onike, Yaba, or any of our branches worldwide (www.mountainoffire.org) and see the manifestation of the power of God that answers by fire to promote you and demote your adversaries.

God bless you richly, as you enter the new year, with the power of a new beginning.

MEETING DAYS AT THE INTERNATIONAL HEADQUARTERS

Day	Service	Time
Sunday	Worship Service	7:00 am
Monday	Spiritual Hospital	5:00 pm
Wednesday	MFM Revival Service	5:00 pm
1st Saturday	Power Must Change Hands	7:00 am (at Prayer City)

Day One
DECEMBER 24 2021

HOLY GHOST, OVERSHADOW ME

Scripture Reading: Luke 1 **Confession:** Luke 4:18

Hymn

1. The God of Abra'am praise
Who reigns enthroned above;
Ancient of everlasting days,
And God of love:
Jehovah, Great I AM,
By earth and heaven confess'd
I bow and bless the sacred name
For ever bless'd.

2. The God of Abra'am praise,
At whose supreme command
From earth I rise, and seek the joys
At His right hand:
I all on earth forsake
Its wisdom, fame, and power;
And Him my only portion make,
My shield and tower.

3. He by Himself hath sworn;
I on His oath depend;
I shall, on eagle's wings upborne,
To heaven ascend;
I shall behold His face,
I shall His power adore;
And sing the wonders of His grace
For evermore.

4. Though nature's strength decay,
And earth and hell withstand,
To Canaan's bounds I urge my way,
At his command
The watery deep I pass,
With Jesus in my view;
And through the howling wilderness
My way pursue.

5. The God, who reigns on high,
The great archangels sing,
And "Holy, Holy, Holy" cry
Almighty King;
Who was and is the same,
And evermore shall be:
Jehovah, Father, Great I AM,
We worship Thee.

6. The whole triumphant host
Give thanks to God on high;
Hail, Father, Son, and Holy Ghost,
They ever cry.
Hail, Abra'am's God, and mine,
I join the heavenly lays;
All might and majesty are Thine,
And endless praise.

Praise and Worship

Prayer Points

1. Thank God for making every evil arrow fired against your life to back fire, in the name of Jesus.
2. Thank God for disengaging the satanic network fashioned against your life in the second heaven and on the earth, in the name of Jesus.
3. The wicked will not succeed in putting me to death, in the name of Jesus.
4. Father, fight all my battles and always give me resounding victory, in the name of Jesus.
5. Unrelenting powers and adversaries working against my life and foundation, expire, in the name of Jesus.

6. Every arrow shot in darkness at me, backfire, in the name of Jesus.
7. Problems, starring me in the face, scatter, in the name of Jesus.
8. Powers sucking the milk of my virtues, vomit them and die, in the name of Jesus.
9. Problems that refuse to shift ground for me, scatter by fire, in the name of Jesus.
10. Powers boasting that I have been defeated, O God, arise and disappoint them, in the name of Jesus.
11. O God, arise and turn the celebration of the enemy over me to tears, in the name of Jesus.
12. Every battle that is bigger than me, O Lord, swallow it, in the name of Jesus.
13. Powers that have increased their instruments of war against me, O Lord, release Your fire to consume them, in the name of Jesus.
14. Powers working hard to keep me in bondage, the Lord rebukes you, in Jesus' name.

Now, make these confessions out loud
1. The Lord will make His face to shine upon me always, and shall be gracious unto me. His light will shine on my path and His favour will encompass me all the days of my life.
2. Associate yourselves, O ye people, and ye shall be broken in pieces; give ear all ye of far countries; gird yourselves, and ye shall be broken in pieces. Take counsel together, it shall come to nought; speak the word, and it shall not stand: for God is with me.
3. When I call upon the name of the Lord, He shall stretch forth His mighty hand and lift me up above all my enemies; and deliver me from all of them, in the name of Jesus.
4. Behold, they that are incensed against me shall be ashamed and confounded: they shall be as nothing; and they that strive with me, shall perish. I shall seek them, and shall not find them, even they that contend with me. They that war against me shall be as nothing.
5. No weapon that is fashioned against me shall prosper, and every tongue that rises against me is already condemned, in the name of Jesus.
6. The sons of those who afflicted me shall come bending low to me; and all those who despised me shall bow down at my feet, in the name of Jesus.
7. When the enemies see the blood, they shall pass over; destroyers will not be able to enter into my house because of the blood of Jesus Christ, in the name of Jesus.

Scripture Reading: Isaiah 37   **Confession:** Isaiah 54:17

Hymn

1. We praise Thee, O God,
   For the Son of Thy love,
   For Jesus who died and
   Is now gone above.

Chorus

   Hallelujah, Thine the glory!
   Hallelujah, Amen!
   Hallelujah, Thine the glory!
   Revive us again.

2. We praise Thee, O God,
   For Thy Spirit of light,
   Who has shown us our Saviour
   And scattered our night.

3. All glory and praise
   To the Lamb that was slain,
   Who has borne all our sins
   And has cleansed ev'ry stain.

4. Revive us again;
   Fill each heart with Thy love;
   May each soul be rekindled
   With fire from above.

Praise and Worship
Prayer Points

1. Thank God for making your Haman to die instead of you, in the name of Jesus.
2. Thank God for the eyes that do not sleep nor slumber that watches over you day and night, in the name of Jesus.
3. Powers assigned to suck me dry, receive instant death, in the name of Jesus.
4. Those who can help me will always arise and help me, in the name of Jesus.
5. I cancel rejection by the power in the blood of Jesus, in the name of Jesus.
6. Every power behind oppression in my life and family, stop your oppression, collapse, and expire, in the name of Jesus.
7. Familiar problems troubling my life, scatter by fire, in the name of Jesus.
8. Familiar battles threatening my existence, lose your power over me, in Jesus' name.
9. Every power sucking life out of me shall perish, in the name of Jesus.
10. Every long-term trouble and long-term affliction that has been prepared for me, expire today, in the name of Jesus.
11. Every power that has pushed me or wants to push me into poverty, die, in the name of Jesus.

12. Wicked elders seeking a way to destroy me shall fail and be disgraced, in the name of Jesus.
13. I frustrate every effort of hell to steal my joy, in the name of Jesus.
14. Every household enemy that has been diverting my glory, I command you to lose your power over me, in the name of Jesus.

Now make these confessions out loud

1. No counsel of the wicked shall stand against me, in the name of Jesus.
2. Unto me shall God do exceeding abundantly above all that I ask, seek, desire and think, according to the power that He had made to work in me, in the name of Jesus.
3. As it is written, I shall be a crown of glory in the hand of God, a royal diadem in the hand of my Maker. I shall begin to shine as a shining light. The light of God is in me.
4. The word of God has made me a brazen wall, a fortified city, an iron pillar. My presence terrifies the enemy. He trembles, feels much pain and travails at the sound of my voice which the Lord has empowered. For it is written, wherever the voice of the king is, there is authority.
5. My appearance is as the appearance of a horse. So, I leap and run like mighty men. When I fall upon the sword, it cannot hurt me, in the name of Jesus.
6. God has equipped me and made me a danger and a terror to all my enemies, in the name of Jesus.
7. The Lord is my light and my salvation, whom shall I fear? The Lord is the strength of my life; of whom shall I be afraid? When the wicked, even mine enemies and foes, came upon me to eat up my flesh, they stumbled and fell, in the name of Jesus.

Scripture Reading: 2 Kings 2   **Confession:** Isaiah 10:27

Hymn

1. O Jesus, I have promised
To serve Thee to the end;
Be Thou forever near me,
My Master and my Friend:
I shall not fear the battle
If Thou art by my side,
Nor wander from the pathway
If Thou wilt be my guide.

2. O let me feel Thee near me,
The world is ever near;
I see the sights that dazzle,
The tempting sounds I hear:
My foes are ever near me,
Around me and within;
But, Jesus, draw Thou nearer,
And shield my soul from sin.

3. O let me hear Thee speaking
In accents clear and still,
Above the storms of passion,
The murmurs of selfwill,

O speak to reassure me,
To hasten or control;
O speak, and make me listen,
Thou Guardian of my soul.

4. O Jesus, Thou hast promised
To all who follow Thee,
That where Thou art in glory,
There shall Thy servant be;
And, Jesus, I have promised
To serve Thee to the end;
O give me grace to follow,
My Master and my Friend.

5. O let me see Thy footmarks
And in them plant mine own;
My hope to follow duly
Is in Thy strength alone,
O guide me, call me, draw me,
Uphold me to the end;
And then in heaven receive me,
My Saviour and my Friend.

Praise and Worship

Prayer Points

1. Thank God for disallowing evil testimonies over your life and family, in the name of Jesus.
2. Thank God for empowering you to defeat the Goliath of your life, in the name of Jesus.
3. Every blessing belonging to me and my family that has been diverted elsewhere, I command those blessings to come back to me and my family now, in the name of Jesus.
4. Every promotion that is supposed to come to me that has been diverted to another person, I command and receive total restoration with compensation now, in the name of Jesus.
5. My glory that has been diverted, I take it back now by the blood of Jesus Christ, in the name of Jesus.
6. Operations of darkness working against my destiny, I disarm you and I command you to catch fire, in the name of Jesus.

7.	Everyone who has sworn that I shall not fulfil my destiny, I decree that your plans have failed, in the name of Jesus.
8.	Every thought of the enemy to make me desert the right path to the wrong path is hereby destroyed by the blood of Jesus Christ, in the name of Jesus.
9.	Every altar of darkness where the spirit of error is assigned against me, I command both the altar and the spirit of error to catch fire, in the name of Jesus.
10.	Every household enemy that has seen my future and wants to divert me from the right path through evil visions, I command you to be destroyed by fire, in the name of Jesus.
11.	I reject every satanic diversion that can push me away from serving Christ, in the name of Jesus.
12.	I reject every evil suggestion made to me by the enemies of my destiny, in the name of Jesus.
13.	I decree that I shall fulfil the glorious destiny for which the enemy is attacking me, in the name of Jesus.
14.	Arrows of depression, I command you to speedily go back and destroy your sender now, in the name of Jesus.

Now make these confessions out loud
1.	The word of God says that God will restore to me, the years that the locust has eaten, the cankerworm, and the caterpillar, and the palmerworm, in the name of Jesus.
2.	With the blood of Jesus, the Lord will flush my land and wash my palms and possessions, in the name of Jesus.
3.	The whole world may decide to go wild with evil flowing like a flood. The enemy, in his evil machinations, may decide against me. The earth may choose not to tremble; whatever may be or happen, I refuse to be shaken, in the name of Jesus.
4.	Who is like unto Him, our God, who dwells on high, far above all powers and dominions. He raiseth up the poor out of the dust, and lifteth the needy out of the dunghill; that He might set him with princes. Even so shall the Lord deal with me, in the name of Jesus.
5.	The Bible says that whatsoever I desire when I pray, I should believe and receive, in the name of Jesus. Therefore, I pray now that, in Jesus' name, I am set free from every captivity or attack of negative speech from my mouth or thoughts and from my heart, against myself.
6.	I tear down, in faith, every spiritual wall of partition between me and my divinely appointed helpers and benefactors, in the name of Jesus.
7.	It is written, "If God be for us, who can be against us?" God is with me; I have no reason to fear, in the name of Jesus.

Day Four
DECEMBER 27 2021

SMITE THE ENEMIES BY THE CHEEK BONES

Scripture Reading: 2 Kings 6   **Confession:** Psalm 3:7

Hymn

1. Ho, my comrades!
   See the signal
   Waving in the sky!
   Reinforcements now appearing,
   Victory is nigh!
   "Hold the fort, for I am coming,"
   Jesus signals still;
   Wave the answer back to heaven,
   "By Thy grace we will."

2. See the mighty host advancing,
   Satan leading on:
   Mighty men around us falling,
   Courage almost gone!

3. See the glorious banner waving!
   Hear the trumpet blow!
   In our Leader's name we'll triumph
   Over ev'ry foe!

4. Fierce and long the battle rages,
   But our help is near:
   Onward comes our great Commander,
   Cheer, my comrades, cheer!

Praise Worship

Prayer Points

1. My Father and my God, I thank You, for You are the Way, the Truth and the Life, in the name of Jesus.
2. My Father, I thank You for being the Bishop of my Soul, in the name of Jesus.
3. Arrows of frustration and anger, I command you to locate your sender and destroy them, in the name of Jesus.
4. You demon called depression, assigned against my life and destiny, I command you to get out of my life by fire, in the name of Jesus.
5. All my enemies, hear the word of the Lord, you must surrender in shame, in the name of Jesus.
6. O Lord, command solution to every difficult situation in my life, in the name of Jesus.
7. O Lord, let my life disgrace every satanic power against me, in the name of Jesus.
8. I declare that every impossible situation is possible, in the name of Jesus.
9. Any door of breakthrough that I have been knocking over the years, open by fire, in the name of Jesus.
10. I curse every trace of poverty in my life, in the name of Jesus.

11. Anyone that has taken anything from me, intending to harm me, be disgraced, in the name of Jesus.
12. O Lord, announce my freedom and breakthroughs from the captives of the spirit of fruitlessness, in the name of Jesus.
13. My Father, cut off every evil tongue cursing my labour, in the name of Jesus.
14. O Lord, arise in Your might and consume by fire every evil spirit stopping me from eating the fruits of my labour, in the name of Jesus.

Now make these confessions out loud

1. I can do and possess all things through Christ who strengthens me. And my God shall supply all my needs according to His riches in glory by Christ Jesus.
2. My heart, from now is comforted, for the God of suddenly, provision and grace is still on the throne, in the name of Jesus.
3. I trust in the word of God. The word stands sure when I speak it. It will accomplish the purpose for which I have spoken it, in the name of Jesus.
4. I am the manifestation, the product and the result of God's word. God has spoken into my life and I have become the manifest presence of Jehovah God on earth. I expressly manifest everything the word of God says I am. I am filled with the word of life.
5. Because the Lord disappointeth the devices of the crafty so that their hands cannot perform their enterprise, every work of the strong, the wicked, the evil and the enemy against my life shall not prosper, in the name of Jesus.
6. In the name of Jesus, I claim the power to overcome all the troops of the enemy.
7. In the name of Jesus Christ, by the presence of God in my life, I command the wicked to perish before me and melt away like wax in the fire.

Scripture Reading: Luke 17

Confession: Matthew 15:26-28

Hymn

1. My times are in Thy hand;
   My God, I wish them there;
   My life, my friends, my soul I leave
   Entirely to Thy care.

2. My times are in Thy hand,
   Whatever they may be,
   Pleasing or painful, dark or bright,
   As best may seem to Thee.

3. My times are in Thy hand;
   Why should I doubt or fear?
   My Father's hand will never cause
   His child a needless tear.

4. My times are in Thy hand,
   Jesus, the crucified!
   Those hands my cruel sins had pierced
   Are now my guard and guide.

5. My time are in Thy hand,
   I'll always trust in Thee;
   And, after death, at Thy right hand
   I shall for eve be.

Praise and Worship
Prayer Points

1. O God, I thank You for You are kind to me when I've been put to shame, in the name of Jesus.
2. O God, I thank You for turning me into an overcomer, in the name of Jesus.
3. O Lord, render the enemies of my life powerless from reaping the fruits of my labour, in the name of Jesus.
4. Anyone that has swallowed snake to harm me, be consumed by fire, in the name of Jesus.
5. Eggs of the serpent in my body, fall out by fire, in the name of Jesus.
6. The water of serpent that I have unconsciously drunk, dry up by fire, in the name of Jesus.
7. Any dark medicine made with any animal against me, catch fire, in the name of Jesus.
8. Any man that has snake poison on his tongue and is cursing me day and night, I command your tongue to dry up, in the name of Jesus.
9. Altar of demonic animals in the house of whosoever is attacking me, catch fire, in the name of Jesus.
10. Whosoever has used money to import different demonic animals to continuously attack, torment and harass me sexually, die by fire, in the name of Jesus.

11. By the heat and fire of the Holy Ghost, let every serpent in my foundation run out and die, in the name of Jesus.
12. Every generational serpent that has taken dominion over my life, be electrocuted and die, in the name of Jesus.
13. Father, silence all my accusers and make ways for me where there seems to be no way, in the name of Jesus.
14. Any day that has been marked for my shame, O Lord, turn it around to be my day of celebration, in the name of Jesus.

Now make these confessions out loud

1. The Spirit of life in Christ Jesus that dwells inside me has delivered me from the law of sin and death including satan, in the name of Jesus.
2. I know by the word of God that, there are many devices in a man's heart; nevertheless the counsel of the Lord shall stand in my life, in the name of Jesus.
3. Jehovah God is all-sufficient. He is more than sufficient. I ask for God's divine abundance in every area of my life and I receive it by faith, in the name of Jesus.
4. I receive unto myself the virtues, the strength, the power, the might and the anointing in the blood of Jesus. And I say, let the blood quicken all that is dead within me. If the enemy comes against me, the Spirit of the Lord will raise up a standard against him and he cannot pass through, in the name of Jesus.
5. No one, principalities, powers, dominions, all of the powers of darkness and even satan himself, can pluck me out of the mighty hand of God; for my God is stronger than all, in the name of Jesus.
6. The Lord will make His face to shine upon me always, and shall be gracious unto me. His light will shine on my path and His favour will encompass me all the days of my life.
7. No weapon that is fashioned against me shall prosper, and every tongue that rises up against me is already condemned, in the name of Jesus.

Scripture Reading: Ezekiel 8   **Confession:** 2 Corinthians 10:4

Hymn

1. Christ our Redeemer died on the cross,
Died for the sinner, paid all his due;
Sprinkle your soul with the blood of the Lamb
And I will pass, will pass over you

   When I see the blood (3 times)
I will pass, I will pass over you.

2. Chiefest of sinners, Jesus will save;
All He has promised, that He will do;
Wash in the fountain opened for sin,
And I will pass, will pass over you.

3. Judgement is coming, all will be there
Each one receiving, justly his due;
Hide in the saving sin cleansing blood
And I will pass, will pass over you.

4. O great compassion! O boundless love!
O loving kindness, faithful and true!
O boundless love! Under the blood,
And I will pass, pass over you.

Praise and Worship

Prayer Points

1. Father, I praise You for being my Hiding Place, in the name of Jesus.
2. Father, I thank You for being my Defender, in the name of Jesus.
3. Every enemy waiting earnestly to laugh at me, I decree that they shall be confounded, in the name of Jesus.
4. Everyone who has sworn that they will not rest until I face reproach, I decree that in a greater measure, the evil you wish for me shall speedily befall you, in the name of Jesus.
5. Powers of darkness monitoring my life to take advantage of any loophole to bring me shame, I command you all to be destroyed by fire now, in the name of Jesus.
6. Altars of darkness established to make me cry in the remaining days of this year, I command you all to be destroyed by the fire of the Lord, in the name of Jesus.
7. Every trap of darkness set for my feet to bring me reproach and shame, I command those who have set the trap to fall into it by themselves, in the name of Jesus.
8. Powers of darkness speaking shame and reproach into my destiny daily, I resist you and I command you to catch fire, in the name of Jesus.
9. Every gift that seems good but is meant to bring me shame, I reject it now, by the blood of Jesus Christ, in the name of Jesus.

10. I frustrate every token of liars concerning my life. As they have gathered to make me see shame, so shall they be scattered, frustrated and confused, in the name of Jesus.

11. Every messenger of darkness hired to make me work in error that I may see shame, I decree your plans have failed by fire, in the name of Jesus.

12. Every evil cycle of shame and disgrace in my family, break by fire, in the name of Jesus.

13. Every loophole in my life that can give the enemy access into my life, Father, by Your mercy, block them off, in the name of Jesus.

14. Every evil personality that has been stationed into my life and surrounded with the mandate to bring me shame, fire of God, drive them far away from me, in the name of Jesus.

Now make these confessions out loud

1. Henceforth, I refuse to live in fear. Rather, my fear and dread shall be upon all my enemies. As soon as they hear of me, they shall submit themselves to me, in the name of Jesus.

2. God wishes above all things that I prosper. I receive prosperity, in the name of Jesus.

3. God has not given me the spirit of bondage to fear. The word of God is quick and powerful in my mouth. God has put the power of His word in my mouth, in the name of Jesus.

4. I am not a failure; I shall operate at the head only and not beneath, in the name of Jesus.

5. I trample under my feet, every serpent of treachery, evil reports, accusations, machinations and criticisms, in the name of Jesus.

6. In the time of trouble, the Lord my God and my Father shall hide me in His pavilion; in the secret places of His tabernacle shall He hide me.

7. With an overrunning flood will the Lord make an utter end of my enemy's habitation, in the name of Jesus.

Scripture Reading: Matthew 1   **Confession:** Matthew 3:16

Hymn

1. From ev'ry stormy wind that blows,
   From ev'ry swelling tide of woes,
   There is a calm, a sure retreat:
   'Tis found beneath the mercy seat.

2. There is a scene where spirits blend,
   Where friends holds fellowship with friend;
   Though sundered far, by faith they meet
   Around one common mercy seat.

3. Ah! Whither could we flee for aid,
   When tempted, desolate, dismayed;
   Or how the hosts of hell defeat,
   Had suff'ring saints no mercy seat.

4. Ah! there on eagle wings we soar,
   And sin and sense molest no more;
   And heav'n comes down our souls to greet,
   While glory crowns the mercy seat.

Praise and Worship
Prayer Points

1. Lord, I give You praise for delivering my soul from death and my feet from stumbling, in the name of Jesus.

2. O God, I thank You because You will be my guide even to the end, in the name of Jesus.

3. Every evil advice from the pit of hell meant to bring me shame in the long run, I reject you now, in the name of Jesus.

4. Evil marks identifying me for evil and spiritual manipulation of demons, blood of Jesus, cancel them, in the name of Jesus.

5. The unknown covenant that has chained me down to the same spot over the years, causing embarrassing situations, break by fire, in the name of Jesus.

6. Planned fountain of problems of the evil ones, instituted against my life, dry up, in the name of Jesus.

7. Circle of the long-term problem around my life, break by fire, in the name of Jesus.

8. Father, let every anti-breakthrough weapon designed against my life be scattered to pieces, in the name of Jesus.

9. O Lord, deliver me from every recurring problem that has refused to let me go, in the name of Jesus.

10. Father, dry up all resources of evil oppressors of my life and destiny, in the name of Jesus.
11. Holy Ghost fire, scatter all evil gang-ups against my life, in the name of Jesus.
12. Father, arise and bring a permanent solution to all long-term problems of my life, in the name of Jesus.
13. Battle of long term problem, assigned to waste me, be terminated now, in the name of Jesus.
14. I frustrate every counsel of hell to delay my journey in this season. It shall not stand, in the name of Jesus.

Now make these confessions out loud

1. I totally trust in the Lord, and I am not leaning on my own understanding. I fill my heart with the words of faith; I receive and speak the words of faith, in the name of Jesus.
2. The young lions do lack and suffer hunger; but I, who seek the Lord God Almighty, shall not lack any good thing, in the name of Jesus.
3. God is my strong Rock and my house of defence, in the name of Jesus.
4. In the name of Jesus Christ, I hand over all my battles to the Lord Jesus Christ. The Lord fights for me and I hold my peace, in the name of Jesus.
5. The Lord has bowed down His righteous ears to deliver me speedily, in the name of Jesus.
6. I shall eat the riches of the Gentiles, and in their glory I shall boast myself, and all shall see and shall acknowledge that I am the seed which the Lord has blessed, in the name of Jesus.
7. I shall no longer be disappointed, or fail at the edge of my desired miracles, success and victory, in the name of Jesus.

New Year Programme

Hymn No. 1 King of Glory, King of Peace

1. King of glory, King of peace,
   I will love Thee;
   And that love may never cease,
   I will move Thee
   Thou hast granted my request,
   Thou hast heard me;
   Thou didst note my working breast,
   Thou hast spare me.

2. Wherefore with my utmost art
   I will sing Thee,
   And the cream of all my heart
   I will bring Thee.
   Though my sins against me cried,
   Thou didst clear me,
   And alone, when they replied,
   Thou didst hear me.

3. Seven whole days, not one in seven,
   I will praise Thee;
   In my heart, though not in heaven,
   I can raise Thee.
   Small it is, in this poor sort
   To enrol Thee;
   E'en eternity's too short
   To extol Thee.

Hymn No. 2

1. All creatures of our God and King
   Lift up your voice and with us sing,
   Alleluia! Alleluia!
   Thou burning sun with golden beam,
   Thou silver moon with softer gleam!
   O praise Him! O praise Him!
   Alleluia! Alleluia! Alleluia!

2. Thou rushing wind that art so strong
   Ye clouds that sail in Heaven along,
   O praise Him! Alleluia!
   Thou rising moon, in praise rejoice,
   Ye lights of evening, find a voice!

3. Thou flowing water, pure and clear,
   Make music for thy Lord to hear,
   O praise Him! Alleluia!
   Thou fire so masterful and bright,
   That givest man both warmth and light.

4. Dear mother earth, who day by day
   Unfoldest blessings on our way,
   O praise Him! Alleluia!
   The flowers and fruits that in thee grow,
   Let them His glory also show.

5. And all ye men of tender heart,
   Forgiving others, take your part,
   O sing ye! Alleluia!
   Ye who long pain and sorrow bear,
   Praise God and on Him cast your care!

6. And thou most kind and gentle Death,
   Waiting to hush our latest breath,
   O praise Him! Alleluia!
   Thou leadest home the child of God,
   And Christ our Lord the way hath trod.

7. Let all things their Creator bless,
   And worship Him in humbleness,
   O praise Him! Alleluia!
   Praise, praise the Father, praise the Son,
   And praise the Spirit, Three in One!

HYMN No. 3

1. O God, our help in ages past,
   Our hope for years to come,
   Our shelter from the stormy blast,
   And our eternal home.

2. Under the shadow of Thy throne
   Thy saints have dwelt secure;
   Sufficient is Thine arm alone,
   And our defence is sure.

3. Before the hills in order stood,
   Or earth received her frame,
   From everlasting Thou art God,
   To endless years the same.

4. A thousand ages in Thy sight
   Are like an evening gone;
   Short as the watch that ends the night
   Before the rising sun.

5. Time, like an ever-rolling stream,
   Bears all its sons away;
   They fly forgotten, as a dream
   Dies at the opening day.

6. O God, our help in ages past,
   Our hope for years to come,
   Be Thou our guard while troubles last
   And our eternal home.

2022 PROSPERITY PRAYER POINTS

Jesus is the Lord of this earth. The earth, with all its fullness, belongs to God. As a joint heir with Jesus, I claim the wealth of this earth, for it belongs to Jesus. I claim all that Jesus' death made available for me to receive. In Jesus' name, I command you devil to lose the wealth of this earth! Take your hands off it now! I command every hindering force against my prosperity to die, in Jesus' name. I bind you, and render you ineffective against me; In Jesus' name. I command wealth, to come to me now! Jesus is the Lord of my life. Jesus is the Lord of my finances. Jesus is Lord!

The Lord is my banker; I shall not owe. He maketh me to lie down in green pastures; He restoreth my losses: He leadeth me beside still waters. Yea, though I walk in the valley of the shadow of debt, I will fear no evil, for thou art with me; thy silver and thy gold, they rescue me. Thou preparest a way for me, in the presence of business competitors; Thou anointed my head with oil, my cup runneth over. Surely goodness and mercy shall follow me all the days of my life, and I shall do successful business, in the name of the Lord. Amen

As God was with Joseph in Potiphar's house and business, so the Lord is with me. As things prospered, in Joseph's hand, so all that I lay my hands upon shall prosper. I will be blessed at home, and I will be blessed in the fields, in the name of Jesus.

My God, has enough riches in heaven in Christ Jesus. Henceforth, I possess the riches of heaven, in Jesus' name.

I have passed through the night of financial crisis. Beginning from today, my morning of joy is starting.

I delight myself in the Word of the Lord. Therefore, I am blessed. Wealth and riches shall be in my house; and my righteousness endureth forever (Ps 112:1-3).

I remember the Lord my God, for it is He that giveth me power to get wealth (De. 8:18.)

With me are riches and honour, enduring wealth and prosperity. (Prov. 8:18.)

I am crowned with wealth. (Prov. 14:24).

I know the grace of my Lord Jesus Christ, that, though He was rich, yet for my sake He became poor, that through His poverty I might be rich (2 Cor. 8:9).

I shout for joy: Let the Lord be magnified, which hath pleasure in the prosperity of His servant (Psalm 35:27).

The Lord is my shepherd (Psalm 23:1).

The Lord prepares a table before me in the presence of my enemies. He anoints my head with oil, my cup runneth over (Psalm 23:5).

The blessing of the Lord makes me rich, and He adds no trouble to it (Prov. 10:22).

I receive wealth from the Lord and the good health to enjoy it (Eccl. 5:19).

I am blessed because I trust in the Lord. I reverence the Lord; therefore, I shall not suffer any lack. The young lions do lack and suffer hunger: But I shall not want any good thing (Psalm 34:8-10).

I have given, and it shall be given unto me, good measure, pressed down, shaken together and running over, shall men give into my bosom. For with the same measure that I mete withal, it shall be measured to me again (Luke 6:38).

God is able to make all grace abound toward me, that I, always having all sufficiency in all things, may have an abundance for every good work (2 Cor. 9:8).

I am prospering in every way. My body keeps well, even as my soul keeps well and prosper (3John 2).

Whatsoever I ask the Father, in the name of His Son Jesus, He will give it to me (John 16:23).

Abraham's blessings are mine (Gal. 3:14).

What things soever I desire, when I pray, I believe that I have received them and I shall have them (Mark 11:24).

I delight myself in the Lord, and He gives me the desires of my heart (Psalm 37:4).

I seek first the kingdom of God; therefore everything I need shall be added unto me (Lk. 12:31).

The wealth of the sinner is laid up for me (Prov. 13:22).

My inheritance shall be forever. I shall not be ashamed in the evil time: and in the days of famine, I shall be satisfied (Psalm 37:18-19).

Every burden shall be taken away from my shoulders, and every yoke from my neck, and the yoke shall be destroyed because of the anointing (Isa. 10:27).

I am like a tree that is planted by the rivers of water. Everything I do shall prosper (Psalm 1:3).

I will not faint, for in due time and at the appointed season, I shall reap if I faint not (Gal. 6:9).

My God, supplies all of my need according to His riches in glory, by Christ Jesus (Phil. 4:19).

There will be no poverty of body, soul and spirit in my life. The anointing of God upon my life gives me favour in the eyes of God and man, all the days of my life. I shall not labour in vain. I shall walk this day in victory and liberty of the spirit.

I bind all evil spirits in me or that are attacking me, in the name of Jesus.

Anything from the kingdom of darkness that has made it its business to hinder me, I single you out right now, and bind you with chains that cannot be broken, in the name of Jesus. I strip off all your spiritual armour, in the name of Jesus. I command you to lose the support of other evil powers, in the name of Jesus. I command you not to involve yourself with me again, in the name of Jesus.

Aggressive Praise and Worship

Prayer Points

1.   O heavens over my prosperity, open by fire, in the name of Jesus.
2.   O God, arise and empower me to prosper, in the name of Jesus.
3.   Every power sitting on my wealth, fall down and die, in the name of Jesus.
4.   Foundational poverty, die, in the name of Jesus.
5.   I take authority over the strong man of financial failure, in the name of Jesus.
6.   I break every covenant of poverty of my father's house, in the name of Jesus.
7.   I enter the covenant of prosperity and abundance with the El Shaddai, in the name of Jesus.
8.   Every curse and covenant responsible for financial embarrassment, I revoke you, in the name of Jesus.
9.   Every evil power that will contest with my voice this year, be silenced, in the name of Jesus.
10. Every power that will contend with my divine destiny this year, scatter, in the name of Jesus.
11. O star of my destiny, arise and shine this year, in the name of Jesus.
12. I silence every strange altar sacrificing my divine opportunities, in the name of Jesus.
13. Blood of Jesus, wipe off all handwriting of failure in my life, in the name of Jesus.
14. Every tree of bad luck, be uprooted by fire, in the name of Jesus.
15. Fire of God, deal with every root of misfortune in my life, in the name of Jesus.
16. When and where others are failing, I shall succeed and I shall get maximum profit, in the name of Jesus.
17. O God, arise and teach me how to make profit, in the name of Jesus.
18. O God, arise and teach me how to produce wealth, even in a bad economy, in the name of Jesus.
19. My Father, breathe upon all I will do this year, in the name of Jesus.
20. Every strong man of failure at the edge of my breakthrough, die, in the name of Jesus.
21. Blood of Jesus, dissolve the root of disgrace in my life, in the name of Jesus.
22. Every witchcraft altar raised against my breakthrough, die, in the name of Jesus.

23. Every ancestral debt collector forcing me to pay for what I did not buy, die, in the name of Jesus.
24. I reject the life of survival on debt. I receive financial breakthroughs to clear my debts, in the name of Jesus.
25. Thou power of family curse and covenant of poverty over my life, break, in the name of Jesus.
26. Those that despised me in the past shall seek my favour, in the name of Jesus.
27. Those who belittled me shall witness my progress, in the name of Jesus.
28. Every cycle of backwardness in my destiny, break, in the name of Jesus.
29. Prosperity terminators in my life, die, in the name of Jesus.
30. Every seed of failure planted in my family line, die, in the name of Jesus.
31. Thou power of aimlessness in my family, die, in the name of Jesus.
32. Lord, anoint my brain to prosper, after the order of Bezaleel, the son of Uri, the son of Hur, of the tribe of Judah, in the name of Jesus.
33. I ask for the release of prosperity into my life, in the name of Jesus.
34. All demonic hindrances to my finances, be totally paralysed, in the name of Jesus.
35. Fire of God, roast all witchcraft bags holding my breakthroughs, in the name of Jesus.
36. Every spiritual satanic bank manager, die, in the name of Jesus.
37. Every dark hand in my foundation, waging war against my destiny, wither, in the name of Jesus.
38. O Lord, let men go out of their ways to show me favour this year, in the name of Jesus.
39. O Lord, let not the lot of the wicked fall upon my life, in the name of Jesus.
40. Every satanic investigation into my future, be dismantled, in the name of Jesus.
41. O Lord, give me the achievement that will swallow my past failures, in the name of Jesus.
42. Every weapon of shame directed against my life, lose your power, in the name of Jesus.
43. Every satanic arrow fired against my star, fall down and die, in the name of Jesus.
44. My destiny, jump out of the pit of debt, in the name of Jesus.
45. Every enemy of my progress, scatter, in the name of Jesus.
46. Every enemy of my miracles, scatter, in the name of Jesus.
47. Thou power of the earth, release my buried virtues, in the name of Jesus.
48. Thou power in the heavenlies, release my captured star, in the name of Jesus.
49. My destiny, reject witchcraft foundation, in the name of Jesus.
50. O Lord, shake down every foundation of hardship in my life, in the name of Jesus.
51. Every blessing that has passed me by, be restored, in the name of Jesus.
52. Every demonic rat eating my prosperity, die, in the name of Jesus.
53. Fire of God, melt away every handwriting of poverty in my life, in the name of Jesus.

COMMAND THE YEAR

Praise and Worship

Scripture Reading - Psalm 91

Confession - Psalm 91

1. This is the year the Lord has made. I will rejoice and be glad in it. I take authority over this year, in the name of Jesus.

2. I decree that all the elements of this year will co-operate with me. I decree that the elemental forces will refuse to cooperate with my enemies. I speak unto the sun, the moon and the stars; they shall not smite me, in the name of Jesus.

3. I pull down every negative energy planning to operate against my life this year. I dismantle any power uttering incantations to capture this year. I render such incantations and satanic prayers null and void. I retrieve this year out of their hands, in the name of Jesus.

4. Spirits of favour, counsel, might and power, come upon me, in the name of Jesus.

5. I shall excel this year and nothing shall defile me. I shall possess the gates of my enemies, in the name of Jesus.

6. The Lord shall anoint me with the oil of gladness above my fellows. The fire of the enemy shall not burn me. My ears shall hear good news, and I shall not hear the voice of the enemy. My future is secured in Christ, in the name of Jesus.

7. God has created me to do some definite services. He has committed into my hands some assignments which He has not committed to anybody. He has not created me for nothing. I shall do good; I shall do His work. I shall be an agent of peace. I will trust Him in whatever I do and wherever I am. I can never be thrown away or downgraded, in the name of Jesus.

8. There will be no poverty of body, soul and spirit in my life this year. The anointing of God upon my life gives me favour in the eyes of God and man, all the days of my life. I shall not labour in vain. I shall walk this year in victory and liberty of the spirit, in the name of Jesus.

9. This year, the Lord will make me an effortless winner and a candidate of uncommon testimonies, in the name of Jesus.

10. This year, I receive my daily bread, good seed to sow every time, and money to spend always, in the name of Jesus.

11. This year, my life will advertise the glory of God, in the name of Jesus.

12. I cancel all appointments with sorrow, tragedy and evil cry this year, in the name of Jesus.

13. This year, I will encounter and experience a full-scale laughter on all fronts, in the name of Jesus.

14. As from now, blood-thirsty demons and robbers will flee at my presence, in the name

of Jesus.

15. Whether I am on the sea, in the air or on the road, evil forces of the world will bow to my authority, in the name of Jesus.

16. Anything I have waited for till now shall be miraculously delivered to me this year, in the name of Jesus.

17. My Father, make me and my family members completely immune to any form of sickness or disease this year, in the name of Jesus.

18. This year, I put myself and members of my family into the protective envelope of divine fire, in the name of Jesus.

19. This year, I will do the will of God, and I will serve God, in the name of Jesus.

20. This year, I will have unconquerable victory, in the name of Jesus.

21. This year, like clay in the hands of a potter, the Lord will make what He wants out of my life, in the name of Jesus.

22. This year, the Lord will do with me whatever He wants, in the name of Jesus.

23. This year, the Lord will make me the head and not the tail, in the name of Jesus..

24. This year, every snare of the fowler assigned against me, shall perish, in the name of Jesus.

25. This year, I render the habitation of darkness, assigned against me desolate, in the name of Jesus.

26. This year, divine deposits shall settle in my life, in the name of Jesus.

27. This year, I enter the covenant of favour, in the name of Jesus.

28. This year, the anointing of success and fruitfulness shall rest on me, in the name of Jesus.

29. This year, I will not be a candidate of sweating without result, in the name of Jesus.

30. This year, all obstacles on my way of progress shall be dismantled, in the name of Jesus.

31. This year, my God shall arise and my stubborn pursuers shall scatter, in the name of Jesus.

32. This year, those that mocked me in the past shall celebrate with me, in the name of Jesus.

33. This year, my Goliath and Haman shall experience destruction, in the name of Jesus.

34. This year, every power assigned to cut short my life shall die, in the name of Jesus.

35. This year, my prayers shall always provoke angelic violence for my good, in the name of Jesus.

36. This year, I shall speak and my words shall bring testimonies, in the name of Jesus.

37. O thou, that troubleth the Israel of the Mountain of Fire and Miracles Ministries, the God of Elijah shall trouble you today, in the name of Jesus.

38. Every enemy of the Mountain of Fire and Miracles Ministries, scatter, in the name of Jesus.

39. O God, arise and uproot anything You did not plant inside the Mountain of Fire and Miracles Ministries, in the name of Jesus.

40. Fire of revival, fall upon Mountain of Fire and Miracles Ministries, in the name of Jesus.

QUENCHING THE RAGE

These prayers are to be prayed between 12:00 am and 12:15 am.

January 7, 2022 - DAY 1
Confessions: Psa. 2:1-12
Aggressive Praise Worship
Prayer Points

1. O Lord, we thank You for the Mountain of Fire and Miracles Ministries, Worldwide, in the name of Jesus.
2. Lord, make this church a citadel of holiness, wonders, miracles and glory upon the earth, marked out by purity, power and progress, in the name of Jesus.
3. Every rage of darkness against the Mountain of Fire and Miracles Ministries, be quenched, in the name of Jesus.
4. Every spirit of mammon working in our church, we bind you, in the name of Jesus.
5. We send the arrow of God upon every power challenging the joy and peace of God, in the lives of the congregation, in the name of Jesus.
6. We cry against the activities of witchcraft powers, water spirits and the queen of heaven in our church, in the name of Jesus.
7. Every satanic police monitoring my life and giving feedback to the kingdom of darkness so they can afflict me, I command you to be destroyed, in the name of Jesus.
8. Every household enemy that has sworn that I shall not have any good thing to celebrate in my life and family, I command you to be exposed and disgraced, in the name of Jesus.
9. The thoughts and evil plans of envious friends shall not excel over my life, in the name of Jesus.
10. My destiny wake up from the satanic altar, in the name of Jesus.
11. O God of Elijah, release fire upon the altar of my enemy, in the name of Jesus.
12. Satanic altar crying against my blood, you are a failure, catch fire, in the name of Jesus.
13. O Lord, keep my altar burning 24 hours of the day, in the name of Jesus.
14. Every stubborn altar feeding on my destiny and future, catch fire, in the name of Jesus.

January 8, 2022 - DAY 2
Confessions: Psa 2:1-12
Aggressive Praise and Worship
Prayer Points

15. You demons of ignorance, working in our church, we bind you; lose your hold and die, in the name of Jesus.
16. Every agenda of the enemy to embarrass the Mountain of Fire and Miracles Ministries, backfire, in the name of Jesus.
17. O God, arise in the thunder of Your power and scatter every warfare assigned against the Mountain of Fire and Miracles Ministries, in the name of Jesus.
18. Every hidden enemy of the Mountain of Fire and Miracles Ministries, be disgraced, in the name of Jesus.

19. Evil altars of my father's house, where are you? Collect your problems back by the blood of Jesus, in the name of Jesus.
20. Any evil done against my destiny so far through the powers of the evil altars, be reversed by the blood of Jesus, in the name of Jesus.
21. My Father, any power making an evil pronouncement on my family names to useless us, O God, arise and turn them to dust, in the name of Jesus.
22. Any ritual done against me at any evil altar by any unfriendly friend, O God, expose them with Your fire, in the name of Jesus.
23. Every satanic priest monitoring my progress from any evil mirror, go blind by fire, in the name of Jesus.
24. My destiny that has just been declared dead by the evil priest, O God, arise and wake it up by fire, in the name of Jesus.
25. The stubborn sacrifice of my father's house that has caged generations, your time is up. burn to ashes and release caged destinies from your altar, in the name of Jesus.
26. O Lord, whenever the evil priest wants to abort my glory, let the thunder of God strike him and his customers to death, in the name of Jesus.
27. Dark powers discussing my destiny in the night season for destruction, receive the arrows of God and die, in the name of Jesus.
28. Satanic laws working against my life, be cancelled now, in the name of Jesus.

January 9, 2022 - DAY 3
Confessions: Psa 2:1-12
Aggressive Praise and Worship
Prayer Points
29. Lord, we pray that MFM will follow its unique calling to fulfill God's purpose for it as a church, in the name of Jesus.
30. You demon of disunity in our church, we come against you. Be bound and die, in the name of Jesus.
31. Every occult demon present in our church, lose your hold. Be bound and die, in the name of Jesus.
32. We bind every attempt of satan to limit the growth of this church qualitatively and quantitatively, in the name of Jesus.
33. Evil trees planted to destroy my destiny, be consumed by fire, in the name of Jesus.
34. Dark river of affliction, flowing into my life from my father's house, dry up by fire, in the name of Jesus.
35. I reject disgrace and I bury all shame and disgrace today, in the name of Jesus.
36. Battles like brass, that refuse to let me go, thunder from heaven, cut them off from me, in the name of Jesus.
37. Spirit of hardship in my life, expire by fire, in the name of Jesus.
38. Father, give me the testimony that will make my enemies praise the God that I serve, in the name of Jesus.
39. I destroy by fire every boundary the enemy has marked down for me, in the name of Jesus.
40. Every spirit that has vowed that I will not move out of this state of poverty and hardship, lose your hold on me, in the name of Jesus.
41. Father, release the chariots of heaven and let them attack and destroy every enemy who has set an array to destroy me, in the name of Jesus.
42. Every bad habit assigned to cut off my glory, be cut off by fire, in the name of Jesus.

January 10, 2022 - DAY 4
Confessions: Psa. 2:1-12
Aggressive Praise and Worship
Prayer Points

43. Every imagination, of unfriendly friends against the Mountain of Fire and Miracles Ministries, scatter, in the name of Jesus.
44. O God, arise and envelop every member of Mountain of Fire and Miracles Ministries with untouchable fire, in the name of Jesus.
45. We bring the judgement of God on every witchcraft power that is afflicting this church, in the name of Jesus.
46. The stronghold, structure and network of wicked men and women in MFM worldwide, collapse, in the name of Jesus.
47. O God of David, arise and deliver me completely from every bad habit, in the name of Jesus.
48. Any bad habit preparing me for doom, perish before you ruin me, in the name of Jesus.
49. Holy Spirit, heal my wounded knee, in the name of Jesus.
50. You the knee of my marriage, receive strength, in the name of Jesus.
51. Everything that is not part of me, begin to vacate my life, in the name of Jesus.
52. Strangers that crept silently into my life, go out by fire, in the name of Jesus.
53. Everything accompanying my work, family and life that is not part of me, go out by fire, in the name of Jesus.
54. O Lord, let the power of spoilers over my life become vain, in the name of Jesus.
55. O Lord, let my spoilers release all their long-term spoils to me, in the name of Jesus.
56. Any dark power that has instigated the devil because of me, let the devil rise against him, in the name of Jesus.

January 11, 2022 DAY 5
Confessions: Psa. 2:1-12
Aggressive Praise and Worship
Prayer Points

57. Every siege against the Mountain of Fire and Miracles Ministries, be dissolved by fire, in the name of Jesus.
58. Every battle from the bottom of the pit to injure the Mountain of Fire and Miracles Ministries, go back to your senders, in the name of Jesus.
59. Every Goliath boasting against the David of Mountain of Fire and Miracles Ministries, fall down and die, in the name of Jesus.
60. According to all that is written in Isaiah 47, we fasten the judgements written therein on the queen of heaven that is responsible for idolatry in our church, in the name of Jesus.
61. Every altar, erected to fight me, catch fire, in the name of Jesus.
62. Any power anointing the devil to fight me, O Lord, arise, fight them, in the name of Jesus.
63. Household altar constantly receiving sacrifices because of me, receive famine, in the name of Jesus.
64. My head, you must not receive the bewitchment of the altar of darkness and its sacrifices, in the name of Jesus.
65. O Lord, let every god put up because of me encounter Your fire, in the name of Jesus.
66. Every strange god, hear the word of the Lord, you will not accomplish any work over me, in the name of Jesus.

67. Every work of the enchanters done to destroy my life, be destroyed, in the name of Jesus.
68. Everyone receiving the offering of enchantment because of me, run mad and die, in the name of Jesus.
69. By the power in the blood of Jesus, no one will be able to curse me, in the name of Jesus.
70. Blessings of Abraham that defies curses, come upon my life, in the name of Jesus.

January 12, 2022 - DAY 6
Confessions: Psa. 2:1-12
Aggressive Praise and Worship
Prayer Points

71. By the blood of Jesus, we break every demonic covenant made between any of our leaders and agents of satan against this church, in the name of Jesus.
72. O Lord, anoint our ministers and pastors like warriors, in the name of Jesus.
73. O Lord, deliver all our pastors, ministers and leaders from satanic distractions, in the name of Jesus.
74. O Lord, deliver the Mountain of Fire and Miracles Ministries worldwide from distractions and stagnation, in the name of Jesus.
75. Everyone embarking on an evil journey to curse me, shall not return, in the name of Jesus.
76. Garments of shame on my body, reducing my honour, tear, in the name of Jesus.
77. Every garment of shame made because of me, O Lord, put it on the maker, in the name of Jesus.
78. O Lord, deliver me; don't let the wicked ones forcefully take my glory from me, in the name of Jesus.
79. Everything I encountered in my father's house, which has increased my battle, O Lord, step on them, in the name of Jesus.
80. What I cannot release willingly to anyone, O Lord, never let anyone be able to take it away from me, in the name of Jesus.
81. Clothes of honour that was removed from my life from the womb, I claim them back, in the name of Jesus.
82. Aged person in my family house that is using my glory to elongate his or her lifespan, die now by fire, in the name of Jesus.
83. My glory and my strength that are being used in the wilderness of slavery in the spirit, come out by fire, in the name of Jesus.
84. Every curse of evil norms that I am being subjected to, O Lord, bring me out, in the name of Jesus.

January 13, 2022 - DAY 7
Confessions: Psa. 2:1-12
Aggressive Praise and Worship
Prayer Points

85. O God, arise, rend the heavens, come down in Your fury and uproot every satanic altar that is speaking against this church, in the name of Jesus.
86. O God arise, come upon this church and overthrow every evil spirit that is afflicting it, in the name of Jesus.
87. Lord, we pray today that unity and family love will not cease in our midst, in the name of Jesus.

88. We pray that, as a church and as individuals, none of our members will miss God's kingdom, in the name of Jesus.
89. My life that is hidden in another person's life, which makes me not understand myself, come out by fire, in the name of Jesus.
90. Heavy evil load tied with my glory, that is preventing my glory from flying, be cut off, in the name of Jesus.
91. Every debt of sacrifice and rituals that my parents owe because of me, blood of Jesus, go and pay it, in the name of Jesus.
92. O God of solutions, sort out my confused life, in the name of Jesus.
93. Whatever was stolen from me, which will not let me act as God created me, O Lord, collect it for me by fire, in the name of Jesus.
94. The idol of my family house that is stealing good things from my life, go into bondage, in the name of Jesus.
95. Every evil resemblance with which I resemble my parents, be disconnected from my life, in the name of Jesus.
96. Covenants that have recreated my destiny, catch fire, in the name of Jesus.
97. My glory, come out of evil markets, in the name of Jesus.
98. O Lord, never allow my portion and destiny to serve as a slave, in the name of Jesus.

January 14, 2022 - DAY 8
Confessions: Psa. 2:1-12
Aggressive Praise and Worship
Prayer Points
99. Blood of Jesus Christ, soak us in You as a church and make us whole, in the name of Jesus.
100. O God, arise and go forth as a mighty Man of war, cry, roar and prevail over the enemies, the strong men, unclean spirits and agents of satan of this church, in the name of Jesus.
101. O God, arise and pass through this church in fury and anger and remove any person who has made a covenant with water spirits or satan to take the seat of Almighty God in this church; let them die the death of the uncircumcised, in the name of Jesus.
102. Revive Thy work, O God in our midst, in the name of Jesus.
103. O Lord, separate my life from people and journeys destined for destruction, in the name of Jesus.
104. O Lord, redeem me from every battle that the fear of my parent sold me into, in the name of Jesus.
105. Every curse or spell that has chosen me as an instrument of vengeance for the error of my parents, blood of Jesus, clear them off, in the name of Jesus.
106. O Lord, destroy every battle growing with my age, in the name of Jesus.
107. Bitter water in my foundation, begin to flow out, in the name of Jesus.
108. Heavenly Father, make me a parent of living children, and never make me weep over my children, in the name of Jesus.
109. O Lord, deliver me from the warrior's error, in the name of Jesus.
110. My honour will not be dishonoured, in the name of Jesus.
111. O Lord, do not allow me to make unpardonable mistakes, in the name of Jesus.
112. Great waters that say I will not cross over, mighty wilderness that says I will not go, Holy Spirit, dry them up, in the name of Jesus.

January 15, 2022 - DAY 9
Confessions: Psa. 2:1-12
Aggressive Praise and Worship
Prayer Points

113. Anything in our lives as a church, that is irritating God, be uprooted by fire, in the name of Jesus.
114. Holy Spirit, fill our members and leaders with Your fire, in the name of Jesus.
115. O God, arise and shake this church. Dethrone those to be dethroned, incapacitate those to be incapacitated, humble those to be humbled, promote those to be promoted and exalt those to be exalted, in the name of Jesus.
116. O God, arise and walk into this church. Whip the profane ministers, moneychangers, selfish and ambitious men, and all that have turned this church to a place of merchandising and showmanship, in the name of Jesus.
117. O Lord, draw me out of every pit of sorrow and trouble, in the name of Jesus.
118. Powers benefiting from my suffering, lose your power over my life, in the name of Jesus.
119. O Lord, never let me use pity to surrender what is precious to me, either physically or spiritually, in the name of Jesus.
120. Every internal battle preparing to open doors to external battles, O Lord, set them ablaze, in the name of Jesus.
121. Every evil river flowing to take away my blessings during sleep or in my dream, dry up by fire, in the name of Jesus.
122. O Lord, shut the door against every weakness in the lives of people that surround me which the devil wants to use to pull me down, in the name of Jesus.
123. Battles that sank the previous warriors, that is preparing to fight me, O Lord, make them sink, in the name of Jesus.
124. Evil occurrences that happened to the previous warriors in my line, and have turned themeselves to a curse, O Rock of Ages, smash them to pieces, in the name of Jesus.
125. O Lord, chase every spirit of Belial out of the people that surround me, in the name of Jesus.
126. Warrior spirit sleeping in me, arise and manifest, in the name of Jesus.

January 16, 2022 - DAY 10
Confessions: Psa. 2:1-12
Aggressive Praise and Worship
Prayer Points

127. Holy Spirit, take over the Mountain of Fire and Miracles Ministries worldwide, in the name of Jesus.
128. Any power of darkness working against the glory of God in the Mountain of Fire and Miracles Ministries worldwide, be destroyed by fire, in the name of Jesus.
129. Every seed and strength of sin in our lives, die now, in the name of Jesus.
130. We prophesy terror and disgrace upon foolish pastors and prophets who are deceiving the flock in this church, in the name of Jesus.
131. Every power or spirit that wants to exchange my warrior glory, be put to shame, in the name of Jesus.
132. Enough is enough! Every rod with which the enemy is flogging me as a warrior, burn to ashes, in the name of Jesus.
133. My battle must not escape. Holy Spirit, fire my battle with poisonous arrows, in the name of Jesus.

134. Battle that prevents good things from lasting long in one's life, O Lord, conquer it for me, in the name of Jesus.
135. O Lord, put in my life today, that which the world will reverence, in the name of Jesus.
136. I rebuke wrong eating and drinking in my life, in the name of Jesus.
137. O Lord, make me worthy of good things, in the name of Jesus.
138. Every battle despising me, perish through the battle of the Holy Spirit, in the name of Jesus.
139. Every load of trouble prepared for my head, O Lord, let my enemy carry it on his head, in the name of Jesus.
140. O Lord, stop me from every dangerous journey; don't let me embark on it again, in the name of Jesus.

January 17, 2022 - DAY 11
Confessions: Psa. 2:1-12
Aggressive Praise and Worship
Prayer Points
141. Every Judas Iscariot around the ministry, family and divine assignment of Dr D. K. Olukoya, Father, expose and disgrace them, in the name of Jesus.
142. Holy Ghost, touch all our youths and teenagers with Your fire, in the name of Jesus.
143. Blood of Jesus Christ, flow through the Mountain of Fire and Miracles Ministries, in the name of Jesus.
144. Father Lord, let every enemy believing he has grown beyond the reach of destruction and judgment in this country, be punished now, in the name of Jesus.
145. Every battle rising against my glory, O Lord, let it work for the breaking forth of my glory, in the name of Jesus.
146. Dry bones in my life, arise and receive fresh power, in the name of Jesus.
147. O Lord, revive me so that the enemy will not fire arrows at me, in the name of Jesus.
148. O Lord, command my head never to trouble me, in the name of Jesus.
149. Bitterness, vacate my life for sweetness to enter, in the name of Jesus.
150. The foundation of the battle troubling my life, be shaken, in the name of Jesus.
151. Secrets of the battles confronting my life, be exposed, in the name of Jesus.
152. Every obstructing enemy, obstructing my life, O Lord, strike them dead and burn them to ashes, in the name of Jesus.
153. Every power of the wicked ones over my life, Son of God, destroy them, in the name of Jesus.
154. My Jesus, the battles in my life is Your battle, trample upon them, in the name of Jesus.

January 18, 2022 - DAY 12
Confessions: Psa. 2:1-12
Aggressive Praise and Worship
Prayer Points
155. O God, arise and let there be stormy wind upon the wicked in this church, in the name of Jesus.
156. O Lord, deliver Your people in this church from the hands of false prophets and pastors, in the name of Jesus.
157. All hiding places of the stubborn enemies of this country, be exposed and shattered to pieces, in the name of Jesus.

158. Satanic pastors/ministers, be disgraced, in the name of Jesus.
159. My Father, my Father, I refuse to continue in the suffering of my parents, in the name of Jesus.
160. I decree, what killed my parents shall not kill me, in the name of Jesus.
161. I refuse to carry the leftover battles of my parents, in the name of Jesus.
162. O Lord, bind strongly, everyone fighting me unknowingly, in the name of Jesus.
163. Everyone doing me harm, O Lord, pay them according to the works of their hands, in the name of Jesus.
164. O Lord, take vengeance on every stubborn pursuer of my life, in the name of Jesus.
165. Every wrong yoke that my generation put upon me, O Lord, remove it from my neck, in the name of Jesus.
166. Every deceptive yoke that is contrary to my life which I am about to put on my neck, O Lord, set it ablaze, in the name of Jesus.
167. Every unequal yoke in my environment, scheming to catch me, scatter by fire, in the name of Jesus.
168. O Lord, deliver me from every wrong yoke that can harm my future, in the name of Jesus.

January 19, 2022 - DAY 13
Confessions: Psa. 2:1-12
Aggressive Praise and Worship
Prayer Points
169. Rebellion against the destiny of this church, be crushed down, in the name of Jesus.
170. We stand against every spirit of marital delay in the lives of our singles, in the name of Jesus.
171. O God, arise and change any profane leader, in this church, in the name of Jesus.
172. O God, arise and wake this church, open the eyes of our understanding, fill us with the knowledge of Your will in all wisdom and spiritual understanding, in the name of Jesus.
173. O Lord, never permit anything that belongs to me to carry the unequal yoke, in the name of Jesus.
174. O Lord, send me back from the path of the unequal yoke for my life, in the name of Jesus.
175. O Lord, pull me out from under the suffering of the unequal yoke, in the name of Jesus.
176. O Lord, expose every unequal yoke that is making me suffer, in the name of Jesus.
177. Weapons of the enemies, vacate my life, in the name of Jesus.
178. O Lord, let the covenant of the wicked ones over my life be misplaced, in the name of Jesus.
179. Strangers in my household, come out by fire, in the name of Jesus.
180. The stumbling spirit will not possess me, in the name of Jesus.
181. O Lord, silence every stumbling voice around me, in the name of Jesus.
182. Power of God that the world does not know its source, enter into my life, in the name of Jesus.

January 20, 2022 - DAY 14
Confessions: Psa. 2:1-12
Aggressive Praise and Worship
Prayer Points
183. O Lord, let Your anointing that produces solution to difficult situations increase upon the Mountain of Fire and Miracles Ministries, in the name of Jesus.

184. Evil mountains challenging this church, be levelled, in the name of Jesus.
185. You strong man, attached to any bad thing currently happening in MFM, be bound and be paralyzed, in the name of Jesus.
186. O God, raise mighty men of valour, faithful pastors and faithful watchmen in this church. Raise a formidable army of the Lord, that will stand in the gap until all cities of the world become a praise on earth, in the name of Jesus.
187. I reject every evil inheritance from my ancestors and parents, in the name of Jesus.
188. The secret to my generational wealth, O Lord, reveal it to me, in the name of Jesus.
189. I receive the power to inherit every inheritance that my ancestors could not use, in the name of Jesus.
190. O Lord, reveal to me what to do that matches my star which will make me break forth, in the name of Jesus.
191. Every destructive ant that grows along with the glory of people in my lineage, fire of God, consume it, in the name of Jesus.
192. Whatsoever will make me great, reveal yourself to me, in the name of Jesus.
193. Standby battle, God needs me, release me, in the name of Jesus.
194. O Lord, send blindness over every besieging battle of my life, in the name of Jesus.
195. O Lord, stop, sack every enemy, every battle besieging my life, in the name of Jesus.
196. O Lord, set ablaze every dark market going on in my body, in the name of Jesus.

January 21, 2022 - DAY 15
Confessions: Psa 2:1-12
Aggressive Praise and Worship
Prayer Points
197. O God, pour Your Spirit upon us and remove all spots, wrinkles, faults, imperfections, filthiness and idols, in the name of Jesus.
198. You hindrance to prayers, we command your forces to break, in the name of Jesus.
199. You stronghold of evil thoughts and imagination against this church, be pulled down, in the name of Jesus.
200. O Lord, discharge and acquit this church from any accusation of the evil ones, in the name of Jesus.
201. Every negative thing that wants to give itself name or change my name; lose your power, in the name of Jesus.
202. Every sickness that wants to hide in me, come out by fire, in the name of Jesus.
203. O Lord, cause my besieging battle and enemies to hear a false alarm and let them be deceived into destruction, in the name of Jesus.
204. Battles that want to make my life, my family and my work desolate, go into the bottomless pit, in the name of Jesus.
205. Henceforth, I am free from the battle of discomfort, in the name of Jesus.
206. O Lord, because of reproach, arise for my help, in the name of Jesus.
207. O God, my age is running, before my family ask where my God is, arise for my help, in the name of Jesus.
208. O Lord, let my besieging battles enter into bondage, in the name of Jesus.
209. Every garment of battle upon me, that wants to humiliate my glory, catch fire, in the name of Jesus.
210. Every spirit of trouble and reproach assigned against me, vacate my environment by fire, in the name of Jesus.

January 22, 2022 - DAY 16
Confessions: Psa. 2:1-12
Aggressive Praise and Worship
Prayer Points
211. Any power that says children of God in this church should not enjoy their lives, let the ground open and swallow them up, in the name of Jesus.
212. All you powers sucking the peace of this church, be bound, in the name of Jesus.
213. Whatever evil that has been agreed upon to be done to this church, we command the evil to be nullified, in the name of Jesus.
214. All the uncalled that are disturbing and oppressing the called, O God, let them see Your hand, in the name of Jesus.
215. Powers that subjected my life to reproach and shame, lose your power, in the name of Jesus.
216. Chains of bondage tying me to wrong or bad source, cut off from my body, in the name of Jesus.
217. You the nature of my glory, come out of bondage and reign as a king, in the name of Jesus.
218. Battles that have swallowed me, vomit me by thunder, in the name of Jesus.
219. Every mark of two steps forward and seven steps backward on my body, Holy Ghost fire, melt it away, in the name of Jesus.
220. O Lord, those that take away good things from someone due to envy, let them not take away good things from me, in the name of Jesus.
221. O Lord, let not my children spoil the work of my hand, in the name of Jesus.
222. Every conspired battle that is united against my life, scatter by fire, in the name of Jesus.
223. Every conspiracy of the wicked ones that wants to erect a tower of battle in my life, O Lord, scatter their language, in the name of Jesus.
224. Every tower of hatred and battle that the enemy is building because of me, scatter by fire, in the name of Jesus.

January 23, 2022 - DAY 17
Confessions: Psa. 2:1-12
Aggressive Praise and Worship
Prayer Points
225. O Lord, ordain terrifying noises in the camp of the enemy of this church, in the name of Jesus.
226. We remove every cloth of shame in this church, in the name of Jesus.
227. O Lord, let the fire of God begin to cause havoc to any evil gathering or association against this church, in the name of Jesus.
228. Mountain of Fire and Miracles Ministries, hear the word of the Lord, you shall not become history while still alive, in the name of Jesus.
229. O Lord, let the habitation of conspirators over my life become desolate, in the name of Jesus.
230. O Lord, use every power inconveniencing my glory as a sacrifice for my glory, in the name of Jesus.
231. O Lord, let people search for me and locate me with my blessings before the end of this year, in the name of Jesus.
232. O Lord, fight for me before my enemies wake up, in the name of Jesus.

233. O Lord, use Your word to deliver me from all bondage, in the name of Jesus.
234. O Lord, use Your word to lift me from my lamed, crippled position, in the name of Jesus.
235. O God, use Your word to glorify Yourself in my life this year, in the name of Jesus.
236. Jesus, Jesus, Jesus, use Your word quickly to bring me to the limelight, so that I won't be lost forever in the wilderness of life, in the name of Jesus.
237. Every enemy that is set to destroy my life, thunder of God, go through the wind to fight them, in the name of Jesus.
238. O God, let the covenant of the wicked elders miss its target over my life, in the name of Jesus.

January 24, 2022 - DAY 18
Confessions: Psa 2:1-12
Aggressive Praise and Worship
Prayer Points
239. You enemies of this country, hear the word of the Lord, you are setting a trap for yourselves, in the name of Jesus.
240. Father Lord, let the wickedness of the wicked, come to an end, in the name of Jesus.
241. Father Lord, seal every miracle you have performed in this church, in the name of Jesus.
242. We reject every evil arrangement concerning this church and receive the arrangement of God, in the name of Jesus.
243. I reclaim all my lost opportunities, in the name of Jesus.
244. Everything that has made me weep, now begin to bring joy and testimonies to me, in the name of Jesus.
245. Every spirit or power using cunningness to take good things away from me, O Lord, crush them, in the name of Jesus.
246. Every power stealing from me with deception and manipulation, Lord, crush them, in the name of Jesus.
247. O Lord, send great trouble to claim back for me everything taken from me in any way, in the name of Jesus.
248. Miracles that will daze my generation, begin to happen in my life, in the name of Jesus.
249. O Lord, satisfy my soul during the season of famine, in the name of Jesus.
250. Every idol of my father's house in my luggage, knowingly or unknowingly, that is chasing away goodness from me, O Lord, set it ablaze, in the name of Jesus.
251. O God of right now, glorify Yourself in my life right now, in the name of Jesus.
252. Garment of glory, that the enemy has mysteriously removed from my body, be returned by fire, in the name of Jesus.

January 25, 2022 - DAY 19
Confessions: Psa. 2:1-12
Aggressive Praise and Worship
Prayer Points
253. Father, in the name of Jesus, let Your Power begin to knock down every strange power within and without the church, in the name of Jesus.
254. O God, arise and pass through the Mountain of Fire and Miracles Ministries worldwide and root out every agent of defilement and pollution, in the name of Jesus.
255. That which the Lord has written concerning this church, you power that has written impossibilities on it, receive the fire of God, in the name of Jesus.

256. Father, let all the evil forces opposing this church begin to rise up against one another, in the name of Jesus.
257. Every evil voice crying for my fall and failure, I reject you, in the name of Jesus.
258. O Lord, never allow the enemy to take away the garment of glory which is Your sign of love upon me, in the name of Jesus.
259. Every spiritual thief hiding in my portion, O Lord, arrest him, in the name of Jesus.
260. Anyone that wants to hurt me with the death of a wife/husband or children, to put out the light of my glory, O Lord, let him harm himself, in the name of Jesus.
261. I refuse anyone to use sweet voice to exchange my portion, in the name of Jesus.
262. I kick out every stranger living with me on the land of my portion, in the name of Jesus.
263. I refuse to ignorantly hand over the treasure of my portion to the enemies, in the name of Jesus.
264. O Lord, use the case of my life to confuse every internal enemy opening the door to the enemy without, in the name of Jesus.
265. O Lord, deliver my glory from dragon-like people and spirits, in the name of Jesus.
266. O Lord, let the host of heaven rise against every dragon power assigned against me, in the name of Jesus.

January 26, 2022 - DAY 20
Confessions: Psa. 2:1-12
Aggressive Praise and Worship
Prayer Points
267. Anywhere evil is being planned against this church, let the consultant and the one consulting receive the fire of God, in the name of Jesus.
268. Spirit of genuine repentance and revival, baptise every member of this church, in the name of Jesus.
269. Any power that will like to attack this church in the night or at anytime, let the ground open up and swallow it, in the name of Jesus.
270. Father Lord, clothe this church with the garment of fire, in the name of Jesus.
271. O Lord, separate me from every dragon power surrounding my life, in the name of Jesus.
272. O Lord, declare Your easy authority upon my life, in the name of Jesus.
273. O Lord, scatter the congregation of Alexander over my life, in the name of Jesus.
274. Every person like Alexander around me, begin to be antagonised, in the name of Jesus.
275. Jesus, let the voice of people like Alexander the coppersmith, around my life be rejected, in the name of Jesus.
276. Jesus, raise voices for me against every person like Alexander and his cohort, in the name of Jesus.
277. O Lord, deliver me from bloodguilt, in the name of Jesus.
278. O Lord, take the curse of bloodguilt away from my head, in the name of Jesus.
279. O Lord, by Your mercy, shut the mouth of every blood crying against me, in the name of Jesus.
280. O Lord, use Your blood to redeem me from every bloodguilt and set me free, in the name of Jesus.

January 27, 2022 - DAY 21
Confessions: Psa. 2:1-12
Aggressive Praise and Worship
Prayer Points

281. You root of impossibilities, be uprooted from this church, in the name of Jesus.
282. Presence of the living God, overshadow the Mountain of Fire and Miracles Ministries worldwide afresh, in the name of Jesus.
283. Father, let there be terror upon every enemy of this church, in the name of Jesus.
284. We destroy the power source of dark powers assigned against Mountain of Fire and Miracles Ministries, in the name of Jesus.
285. O Lord, reveal Your mightiness over the battle of my life, in the name of Jesus.
286. Longtime battles, come out of my life, in the name of Jesus.
287. Every power that says my vine will not grow, O Lord, destroy it by fire, in the name of Jesus.
288. Every spirit that has been influenced to soil my tender plants, O Lord, consume it with fire, in the name of Jesus.
289. Every power that has been given the assignment to spoil my tender plants, O Lord, fire him with the arrow of death, in the name of Jesus.
290. My tender plants shall not welcome death, in the name of Jesus.
291. Every conspiracy to spoil the tender plants of my work, family and ministry, I scatter it, in the name of Jesus.
292. Every battle growing with my tender plants, come out by fire, in the name of Jesus.
293. I reject the death of any tender plants in my life, in the name of Jesus.
294. Any assassin of tender plants in my environment, O Lord, let him lose his life, in the name of Jesus.

January 28, 2022 - DAY 22
Confessions: Psa. 2:1-12
Aggressive Praise and Worship
Prayer Points

295. Every anti-heaven spirit within the church, get out, in the name of Jesus.
296. Lord, increase in the lives of our members and pastors; help us to know You more, in the name of Jesus.
297. Father Lord, convert the prayers of this church to fire; and wherever it goes, let it perform its purpose, in the name of Jesus.
298. Father, let every spiritual and physical blessing of this church, be released, in the name of Jesus.
299. The sword of God that is protecting the Garden of Eden, begin to protect my tender plants, in the name of Jesus.
300. My tender plants, receive courage and boldness against every wind and whirlwind of the world, in the name of Jesus.
301. Every evil calabash that is being used to monitor the future of my tender plants, break by fire, in the name of Jesus.
302. My tender plants shall not weep, in the name of Jesus.
303. I refuse to bury my tender plants, in the name of Jesus.
304. Every arrow of stunted growth fired into my tender plants, come out by fire and go back to your sender, in the name of Jesus.

305. Every arrow of incessant sickness programmed into my tender plants, die by fire, in the name of Jesus.
306. Every devourer in the land where my tender plants are planted, fire of God, begin to consume it, in the name of Jesus.
307. Every price of darkness required for the breakthrough of my tender plants, blood of Jesus, pay it off, in the name of Jesus.
308. The vehicle of an accident shall not enter into the garden where my tender plants are planted, in the name of Jesus.

January 29, 2022 - DAY 23
Confessions: Psa. 2:1-12
Aggressive Praise and Worship
Prayer Points
309. Every power boasting against the prayers of this church, we command such power to bow, in the name of Jesus.
310. Father, give all our members and pastors hunger for righteousness and godliness, in the name of Jesus.
311. O Lord, cause it to happen, that the failure of the devil will advance in this church, in the name of Jesus.
312. Father Lord, make the spiritual life of every member of MFM to be too hot for the enemy to handle, in the name of Jesus.
313. O Lord, reveal Your mightiness over the battle of my life, in the name of Jesus.
314. People will celebrate the favour of God with me this month, in the name of Jesus.
315. Anointing of the Lord Almighty, begin to flow upon my life, in the name of Jesus.
316. Healing anointing, rest upon my life, in the name of Jesus.
317. The anointing to perform my responsibilities, rest upon my life, in the name of Jesus.
318. The anointing that makes one prosper amidst one's enemies, rest upon my life, in the name of Jesus.
319. The anointing that no one can conspire against, rest upon my life, in the name of Jesus.
320. The anointing that draws favour upon a man, O Lord, release it upon my life, in the name of Jesus.
321. The anointing that makes one glitter, O Lord, pour it upon my life, in the name of Jesus.
322. The anointing that makes one become king, O Lord, pour it upon my life, in the name of Jesus.
323. The anointing that distinguishes, O Lord, pour it upon my life, in the name of Jesus.

January 30, 2022 - DAY 24
Confessions: Psa. 2:1-12
Aggressive Praise and Worship
Prayer Points
324. Father, let the Angel of God hinder and stop all the works of darkness in this church, in the name of Jesus.
325. O Lord, quench all foreign fire in this church and put Your own fire in it, in the name of Jesus.
326. We pull down all the strongholds of evil strangers in this church, in the name of Jesus.
327. We cancel all the effects of evil marks in the lives of the congregation, in the name of Jesus.

328. All my tender plants that have been arrested, O Lord, the Great Deliverer, liberate them, in the name of Jesus.
329. I shall eat the fruits of my tender plants, in the name of Jesus.
330. Every thorn that is choking my tender plants, wind of the Almighty God, uproot and sweep them away, in the name of Jesus.
331. My tender plants, receive divine water from above, in the name of Jesus.
332. Daily dew, fall upon my tender plants, in the name of Jesus.
333. Every poison that was used in the foundation of my tender plants, blood of Jesus, flush it out, in the name of Jesus.
334. O Lord, plant my tender plant in the land of peace, in the name of Jesus.
335. My tender plants, receive the mark of favour, in the name of Jesus.
336. Every dangerous and envious person that is envious of the development of my tender plants, destroy yourselves, in the name of Jesus.
337. My tender plants, receive the untouchable and unbeatable power of God, in the name of Jesus.

January 31, 2022 DAY 25
Confessions: Psa 2:1-12
Aggressive Praise and Worship
Prayer Points
338. We command all the demonic animals sent to any member of the congregation by household enemy, to receive thunder judgement of God, in the name of Jesus.
339. We command all evil spiritual eyes that are looking into the lives and progress of the congregation to receive blindness, in the name of Jesus.
340. We stand against every form of tragedy in the lives of the congregation, in the name of Jesus.
341. We stand against every power that pushes people into hell in the midst of the congregation, in the name of Jesus.
342. O Lord, take strength and power away from my oppressors, in the name of Jesus.
343. Rock of salvation, arise, hit my enemy, and deliver me from their hands, in the name of Jesus.
344. Where my oppressors hang the finished work of my life, O Lord, enter into the place and destroy the work, in the name of Jesus.
345. All my comforters that are tied down that is making me remain in problem, O Lord, go and set them free, in the name of Jesus.
346. Every evil title ascribed to me, blood of Jesus, rub it off, in the name of Jesus.
347. Evil occurrences that occur to people of God, my portion rejects it, in the name of Jesus.
348. In all the days and years that I will spend on earth, O Lord, do not allow what is supposed to be unheard of concerning children of God to happen to me, in the name of Jesus.
349. Evil shall not be heard of me, in the name of Jesus.
350. Every sin that can bring me down from victory, O Lord, forgive me, in the name of Jesus.
351. Every sin, iniquity and trespass that may make me not to go from victory to victory, O Lord, forgive me, in the name of Jesus.

February 1, 2022 - DAY 26
Confessions: Psa. 2:1-12
Aggressive Praise and Worship
Prayer Points

352. Every spiritual barrier and limitation, to success, in the lives of the congregation, we command it to break into pieces, in the name of Jesus.
353. We command all the seeds of failure in the lives of the congregation to be consumed by the fire of God, in the name of Jesus.
354. We stand against every power that pushes people into error in the midst of the congregation, in the name of Jesus.
355. Every spiritual barrier and limitation, to progress, in the lives of the congregation, break into pieces, in the name of Jesus.
356. O Lord, make me a warrior at the battlefront, in the name of Jesus.
357. From the battlefront, I shall come home with trophies, in the name of Jesus.
358. O Lord, let the spirit of a warrior and the spirit of a conqueror at the battlefront possess me, in the name of Jesus.
359. O Lord, give me the power of a warrior and anoint me with the oil of a warrior, in the name of Jesus.
360. O Lord, make me a warrior both in my sleep and in the dreamland, in the name of Jesus.
361. O Lord, let the spirit of courage in danger possess me, in the name of Jesus.
362. O Lord, make me stand in Your power, in the name of Jesus.
363. O Lord, never allow me to rely on my power, in the name of Jesus.
364. The spirit that prays and watches, let it rest upon me, in the name of Jesus.
365. Where the work and danger call, O Lord, empower me to get there, in the name of Jesus.

February 2, 2022 - DAY 27
Confessions: Psa. 2:1-12
Aggressive Praise and Worship
Prayer Points

366. We command all agents of failure in the lives of the congregation to be consumed by the fire of God, in the name of Jesus.
367. Father Lord, let the wind of the Holy Spirit blow in His fullness into the lives of the congregation, in the name of Jesus.
368. We stand against the spirit of broken homes in the lives of the congregation, in the name of Jesus.
369. We stand against every business attack and financial failure in the lives of the congregation, in the name of Jesus.
370. The crown of a conqueror and weapons of a conqueror, O Lord, give them to me, in the name of Jesus.
371. Where the enemy is standing to prevent good things from entering my life, fire of God, chase him out, in the name of Jesus.
372. Where my enemy is camping to send away my blessings, Lord, chase him away with fire, in the name of Jesus.
373. Anyone in my camp who is the chief of my battle, O Lord, separate us by fire, in the name of Jesus.
374. Anyone standing on the way through which good things are supposed to pass into my life

and home, fire of God, clear him away, in the name of Jesus.

375. The junction at which my hinderer is standing against my life, authority of fire, remove them, in the name of Jesus.
376. O Lord, let goodness begin to enter into my life and home, in the name of Jesus.
377. O Lord, let Your spirit rest on me whenever I encounter lions that want to stop me or take me backward in life, in the name of Jesus.
378. O Lord, silence every lion for me, in the name of Jesus.
379. I shall trample upon every lion-like person, in the name of Jesus.

February 3, 2022 - DAY 28
Confessions: Psa. 2:1-12
Aggressive Praise and Worship
Prayer Points

380. We stand against every attack by evil spirits in the lives of the congregation, in the name of Jesus.
381. Anything making the promises of God to fail in the lives of the congregation, O Lord, we cancel them with the blood of Jesus, in the name of Jesus.
382. Lord, let Your divine favour be upon every member of the congregation, in the name of Jesus.
383. We command anything that hinders every member of the congregation from their blessing to give way, in the name of Jesus.
384. Every ancient door that anyone has locked against me, be opened and scattered, in the name of Jesus.
385. O Lord, let my fullness of time come that I may enter into my glory, in the name of Jesus.
386. Holy Spirit, let the fullness of time that my enemies would release me come, in the name of Jesus.
387. God of the fullness of time, let my bondage and sorrow expire, in the name of Jesus.
388. O Lord of the fullness of time, liberate me, in the name of Jesus.
389. God of the fullness of time, let the covenant of fullness of time come to work in my life, home and work, in the name of Jesus.
390. What heaven has recorded in my destiny, my marriage and work, begin to manifest, in the name of Jesus.
391. The wealth of my work and ministry, come forth, in the name of Jesus.
392. Every good thing that I am due for, begin to come forth, in the name of Jesus.
393. O Lord, make me important and valuable on earth, in the name of Jesus.

February 4, 2022 - DAY 29
Confessions: Psa. 2:1-12
Aggressive Praise and Worship
Prayer Points

394. We take authority over the strong man in the lives of the congregation, in the name of Jesus.
395. Every gathering, being held in the air, in the ground, in the forest and in the second heaven against the lives of the congregation, scatter, in the name of Jesus.
396. Father, let the dark forces hiding the blessings of the congregation release them, in the mighty name of Jesus.
397. O Lord, convert the burdens in the lives of the congregation to blessings, in the name of Jesus.

398. O Lord that made Daniel valuable in the land of Babylon, make me valuable on earth, in the name of Jesus.
399. O Lord that made Paul a valuable person to the heathens, make my ministry valuable in the world, in the name of Jesus.
400. The virtue that will make my name great in life, O Lord, pour it upon my life, in the name of Jesus.
401. Jesus, make me a blessing for the countries in the world, in the name of Jesus.
402. O Lord, make me indispensable in the world, in the name of Jesus.
403. Every thief standing in my way, Holy Spirit, encounter them with fire, in the name of Jesus.
404. Every junction that darkness is staying to steal or snatch good things from me, O Lord, pass through it with fire, in the name of Jesus.
405. Every thief constantly stealing from me, their battle ends today, in the name of Jesus.
406. Every good gift You have given me, O Lord, clothe it with the garment that can never be spoilt, in the name of Jesus.
407. O Lord, every good thing that You will do for me must be long lasting, in the name of Jesus.

February 5, 2022 - DAY 30
Confessions: Psa. 2:1-12
Aggressive Praise and Worship
Prayer Points
408. O Lord, remove the garment of sickness from the lives of the congregation, in the name of Jesus.
409. Father Lord, let my enemies be confounded and troubled, in the name of Jesus.
410. O Lord, remove the garment of debt from the lives of the congregation, in the name of Jesus.
411. O Lord, remove the garment of death and sorrow from the lives of the congregation, in the name of Jesus.
412. My expectations must not be polluted again, in the name of Jesus.
413. Every power elongating my expectations, receive destruction, in the name of Jesus.
414. Every power destroying my expectations, receive the sword of fire, in the name of Jesus.
415. This month, bring forth my expectations, in the name of Jesus.
416. My expectations, begin to become flesh, in the name of Jesus.
417. O Lord, search and locate me from where I am not supposed to be, in the name of Jesus.
418. Whatever that is tying me down in a wrong place, O Lord, disconnect it from me, in the name of Jesus.
419. Every stumbling block or barrier leading me to the wrong path, O Lord, remove them, in the name of Jesus.
420. Holy Spirit, lead me to my promised land, in the name of Jesus.
421. O Lord, draw me out from the pit of misdirection, in the name of Jesus.

February 6, 2021 - DAY 31
Confessions: Psa. 2:1-12
Aggressive Praise and Worship
Prayer Points
422. Every tree that fear has planted in the lives of the congregation, be uprooted, in the name of Jesus.

423. You power of the wasters, release the spiritual power of every member of the congregation, in the name of Jesus.
424. O Lord, let the Holy Ghost fire, melt away whatsoever is blocking the spiritual pipe line of the congregation, in the name of Jesus.
425. O Lord, let the spirit of slumber, spirit of forgetfulness and spirit of confusion, depart from the lives of the congregation, in the name of Jesus.
426. O Lord, call forth my next miracles, in the name of Jesus.
427. O Lord, raise agents of miracles for me, in the name of Jesus.
428. O Lord, help me where I have been rejected, in the name of Jesus.
429. O Lord, conquer every battle scaring my helpers away, in the name of Jesus.
430. O Lord, let me not be sent on an evil errand with a heavy load, in the name of Jesus.
431. Every door of sorrow opened before me and my family, O Lord, shut it up, in the name of Jesus.
432. O Lord, never permit the enemies to replace my joy with tears, in the name of Jesus.
433. O Lord, uproot every bitterness planted into my life by the enemies, in the name of Jesus.
434. O Lord, conquer the battle of glory afflicters in my life, in the name of Jesus.
435. O Lord, deliver me from anyone raising battle because of my glory, in the name of Jesus.

February 7, 2021 - DAY 32
Confessions: Psa. 2:1-12
Aggressive Praise and Worship
Prayer Points
436. You powers that turn the lives of the people to dustbin, in the lives of the congregation, be bound, in the name of Jesus.
437. Every arrow of prayerlessness, fired into the congregation by the enemy, go back to the senders, in the name of Jesus.
438. O Lord, envelop every member of the congregation in Your glory, in the name of Jesus.
439. Every coffin prepared by the agent of death for my life, catch fire and roast to ashes, in the name of Jesus.
440. Every evil work my home town and my environment are doing over my glory, catch fire, in the name of Jesus.
441. The wonder that will make the world believe in my God, O Lord, do it in my life, in the name of Jesus.
442. Strange spirits quenching the fire of good things in my life, enter into bondage, in the name of Jesus.
443. O Lord, redeem me from every valley of limitation I have been thrown into, in the name of Jesus.
444. O Lord, let my testimonies turn around for good, in the name of Jesus.
445. O Lord, with Your power, remove me from every graveyard I have been kept, in the name of Jesus.
446. Battles that are above me, hindering me from being seen, O Lord, humble them, in the name of Jesus.
447. Every battle that my parents didn't conquer and has become a battle for me, O Lord, conquer it today, in the name of Jesus.
448. Resemblance battles in my life, catch fire, in the name of Jesus.
449. O Lord, never allow sorrow to share out of my days of joy, in the name of Jesus.

CRY AGAINST THE SPIRIT O F SENNACHERIB

Praise and worship

Scripture Reading - Isaiah 37

Confession - Psalm 18:29

1. O God arise and uproot anything You did not plant, inside the Mountain of Fire and Miracles Ministries, in the name of Jesus.

2. O God, let the fire of revival fall upon the Mountain of Fire and Miracles Ministries, in the name of Jesus.

3. O God, let the power of peace and progress, overshadow this nation, in the name of Jesus.

4. O God, arise and give us God-fearing leaders, in the name of Jesus.

5. Any power standing by me and has vowed to wage war against me. O Lord, wage war against him, in the name of Jesus.

6. Powers, assigned to turn the source of my joy to a source of sorrow, O God, arise and wage war against them, in the name of Jesus.

7. Wicked power using the spirit of hatred to wage war against me, O Lord, wage war against him, in the name of Jesus.

8. Battle of hatred assigned to replace the day of my joy, be consumed by fire, in the name of Jesus.

9. Wicked powers, using the spirit of hatred to wage war against my glory, the Lord rebuke you, in the name of Jesus.

10. O Lord, chase away the spirit of hatred from my destiny, in the name of Jesus.

11. Wherever the wicked one has stopped me, I go beyond that place, in the name of Jesus.

12. Spirit of witchcraft that allows one's effort to be wasted, fire of God, chase them out of my life, in the name of Jesus.

13. Wretchedness in my destiny, be consumed by fire, in the name of Jesus.

14. Spirit of 'working without reward' in my life, catch fire, in the name of Jesus.

15. Every unseen kingdom that says I should keep working in vain, lose your kingdom by fire, in the name of Jesus.

16. You kingdom of darkness holding my life, O Lord, scatter it, in the name of Jesus.

17. O Lord, snatch the kingdom of my life from the hands of the wicked ones, in the name of Jesus.

18. Wicked hands assigned to steal my garment of mercy, be consumed by fire, in the name of Jesus.

19. Intervention of darkness assigned to make me lose my blessings, shut up by fire, in the name of Jesus.

20. Powers working to keep me in bondage, perish by fire, in the name of Jesus.

21. Evil conspiracies assigned to displace me and put me to shame, be scattered, in the name of Jesus.

22. Every dark force opposing my rising, die, in the name of Jesus.

23. Agents of darkness conniving to kill my shining, I throw confusion into your midst, scatter, in the name of Jesus.

24. Every oppressing and opposing force, the Lord rebuke you, in the name of Jesus.

25. Favour that divinely selects and lifts up, come upon my life, in the name of Jesus.

26. Dark forces assigned to make me rotate on one spot, die by fire, in the name of Jesus.

27. Thunder from heaven, strike and electrocute unrelenting pursuer of my destiny, in the name of Jesus.

28. Axe of God, destroy the agenda, covens and habitation of household witches, in the name of Jesus.

29. Deep incantations and evil arrows from my father's and mother's houses, go back to senders, in the name of Jesus.

30. Evil winds from the prince of the power of the air, be still, die, in the name of Jesus.

31. Spiritual and physical thieves, give up what you have stolen from me and my family by the power in the blood of Jesus, in the name of Jesus.

32. Battles making my case difficult, scatter by fire, in the name of Jesus.

33. Every good thing that is about to die in my life and destiny, receive life by the resurrection power in the blood of Jesus, in the name of Jesus.

34. Sudden problem arising against my destiny, I silence you, in the name of Jesus.

35. Rage of destruction targeted at my life and destiny, scatter, in the name of Jesus.

36. Powers enforcing wickedness against my life and family, expire, in the name of Jesus.

37. Every visitation meant to derail me and demote me, expire, in the name of Jesus.

38. Destruction of good things in my life and future, come to an end, in the name of Jesus.

39. Raging waves against me, I command you, be still, in the name of Jesus.

40. The lying-in-wait of the wicked for me shall turn to disappointment, in the name of Jesus.

Made in the USA
Monee, IL
21 December 2021

86734218R00026